Published by
Celestial Enterprises
3645 Marketplace Blvd. Ste 130-785, East Point, Ga 30344

THIS JOURNAL BELONGS TO:

_____

> **"**
> You are uniquely fashioned with creativity, quirkiness and intellect that makes you special and awesome at the same time. Embrace, Maximize and then Monetize it. The only thing stopping and limiting you is YOU. **"**

Your Biggest Cheerleader
Coach T, College Prep Boss™

This planning guide was created to make you a Money Magnet who gets:

Noticed for your accomplishments in leadership, academics and community service

Admitted into colleges who will facilitate the manifestation of your vision and dreams

Funded with scholarship dollars with zero to very little student loan debt

Opportunities that create options; and options that yield many opened doors so you are never limited and left without choices.

Who Am I?

First, she is a first-generation college graduate and your biggest cheerleader!

Many know her as the College for Free® Coach and College Prep Boss™ with many accolades. An award-winning, multi-bestselling author, international trainer, speaker, coach, and Executive Leadership Strategist specializes in developing youth and leaders. Roles include being a member of the Forbes Coaches Council, John Maxwell Team, and an Adjunct Professor. At the same time, you will find her work in the Huffington Post, Examiner, Lifetime Moms, and other media outlets. Radio Personality Sasha the Diva recently identified Ms. Williamson as a Divas Diamonds for her work with high-school families to avoid student loan debt.

As a College Prep Boss™, Ms. Williamson served as the resident College Admissions and Funding Coach for several organizations, such as the Urban League of Atlanta, Usher's New Look Foundation, Atlanta CARES, and many more. Through her work, she has touched over 5000 students and helped clients garner over $40 Million in scholarships and receive acceptance into top-tier institutions like UPenn, UCLA, Stetson, Dartmouth, Howard, and many more. This is why Tameka is known as The College Prep Boss™. Her mission is all about helping students attend college without any debt.

Tameka, a transformational leader, and College Prep Boss™ want you to not only Get Ready but always Be Ready and learn to Stay Ready. This is the key to being a Money Magnet.

JOIN OUR FACEBOOK COMMUNITY

f www.facebook.com/college4free

Learn more about becoming a Money Magnet by connecting with us and joining the community

Create a Short Video or Fun Post Showing how you completed the planner or benefited from the use of the planner on any of our social media networks, tag us and use hashtag **#GettingAFullRide** for a chance to win a prize.

instagram.com/iamcoachtwill

Youtube.com/CoachTwill

crushcollegedebt.com

Foundation

Understand the basics and build a foundation you can capitalize on. With that, you must also understand basic information regarding the college admissions process.

"OUR GOALS CAN ONLY BE REACHED THROUGH A VEHICLE OF A PLAN, IN WHICH WE MUST FERVENTLY BELIEVE, AND UPON WHICH WE MUST VIGOROUSLY ACT. THERE IS NO OTHER ROUTE TO SUCCESS."

Pablo Picasso

Goal Setting

One action an intentional leader does is set goals for themselves prior to creating a plan and strategy for getting it done. Here we are challenging you to define and set goals for yourself, your life, and future. Goals are commonly defined for personal, health, academic, business, career, and family reasons.

Then you want to make sure you set SMARTR goals.

S – specific: state what you will do (use action words)

M – measurable: use metrics or data to evaluate your goal

A – attainable/achievable: it's within your scope/wheelhouse

R – realistic: it's possible for you to achieve it

T – timely: name exactly when you want to accomplish it

R – relatable: it's connected to your purpose, vision and/or mission

Instructions: To help provoke thought around areas you can set goals, answer the questions below. Be specific, open and honest with yourself. Then detail what your plan of action will be for getting it done.

Personal Goals: This category of goals puts the focus on you as a person. So, you are going to explore goals that relate to your personal relationships and help you improve your self- image, enhance creativity, intellectual abilities, and shift your attitude/mindset.

1   What attitudes or beliefs about yourself would you like to change or improve? How and when will you go about doing this?

2   What self-limiting thoughts or fears would you like to overcome? What steps will you take to overcome them?

3   What personality trait(s), such as being more dependable/responsible, would you like to cultivate, eliminate or better manage? How can you do this?

4   What dreams, hopes, visions and/or designs do you have for yourself? What steps can you take to make this a reality?

5   What habits are you not happy with and/or you find are not productive in your life? What will you do to change them?

Based on your answers to the questions, list the most critical goals you would like to focus on first. Then rank their level of priority as High, Medium or Low. Think of your goals in terms of Short-Term (1—90 days), Mid-Range (3—12 months) and Long-Term (1—5 years) and identify them as such. Remember, goals must be SMARTR.

Goal 1:

Goal Category (personal, academic, etc):

Type of Goal (short, mid-range, long-term):

How is it:

Specific:

Measurable:

Attainable:

Realistic:

Timely:

Relatable:

Goal 2:

Goal Category (personal, academic, etc):

Type of Goal (short, mid-range, long-term):

How is it:

Specific:

Measurable:

Attainable:

Realistic:

Timely:

Relatable:

Goal 3:

Goal Category (personal, academic, etc):

Type of Goal (short, mid-range, long-term):

How is it:

Specific:

Measurable:

Attainable:

Realistic:

Timely:

Relatable:

Goal 4:

Goal Category (personal, academic, etc):

Type of Goal (short, mid-range, long-term):

How is it:

Specific:

Measurable:

Attainable:

Realistic:

Timely:

Relatable:

Goal 5:

Goal Category (personal, academic, etc):

Type of Goal (short, mid-range, long-term):

How is it:

Specific:

Measurable:

Attainable:

Realistic:

Timely:

Relatable:

EDUCATIONAL GOALS

This category focuses on your education in areas of grades, training, schooling and certifications. These goals are meant to help you challenge yourself to improve your current educational level and strive for something higher.

What GPA would you like to have on your report card in middle school, high school, and/or college? How will you go about achieving this?

What clubs, organizations or sports would you like to join and excel in? What will you do to accomplish this?

What score would you like to get on your PSAT, ACT and/or SAT? What will you do to accomplish this?

What do you want to achieve in your education (Dean's List, Honor Society, Valedictorian, etc.)? How will you go about making this a reality?

What degrees would you like to attain (Associate, Bachelor's, Master's, and Doctorate)? How will you accomplish this?

Goal 1:

Goal Category (personal, academic, etc):

Type of Goal (short, mid-range, long-term):

How is it:

Specific:

Measurable:

Attainable:

Realistic:

Timely:

Relatable:

Goal 2:

Goal Category (personal, academic, etc):

Type of Goal (short, mid-range, long-term):

How is it:

Specific:

Measurable:

Attainable:

Realistic:

Timely:

Relatable:

Goal 3:

Goal Category (personal, academic, etc):

Type of Goal (short, mid-range, long-term):

How is it:

Specific:

Measurable:

Attainable:

Realistic:

Timely:

Relatable:

Goal 4:

Goal Category (personal, academic, etc):

Type of Goal (short, mid-range, long-term):

How is it:

Specific:

Measurable:

Attainable:

Realistic:

Timely:

Relatable:

Goal 5:

Goal Category (personal, academic, etc):

Type of Goal (short, mid-range, long-term):

How is it:

Specific:

Measurable:

Attainable:

Realistic:

Timely:

Relatable:

Career

The goal of researching potential careers and its corresponding job potential is to one find a career path that yields opportunities post-college. Secondly, we want to help you avoid picking a field that yields zero ROI and/or opens the door for you to change your major. Either option results in wasted money and time and an unfulfilled life.

Finding the *Right Career*

What careers are you interested in?

List the careers and their educational requirements and the skills needed to work in each career field

Based on job forecast data, what does the job matket look like for each career field? what geographical location has the highest demand or job opportunities? (refer to this chapter in College for FREE book)

Make note of other details discovered about your career of interest

Do you know of anyone who works in the career fields of interest? If yes, list them and create a task to interview them and discuss your findings. If not, tap into your network to identify a person to interview

Based on your findings, what steps do you need to take to prepare yourself better for your desired career choice?

General Notes:

Career Goals:

This category deals with preparing for, enhancing and/or improving your career and professional achievements. These goals can be centered around starting your own business, achieving a certain position or even obtaining certain certifications.

What leadership skills would you like to strengthen? How will you do it?

What professional skills would you like to enhance (public-speaking, presentations, etc.)

What specific things can you do change, or eliminate to become more organized and productive How will you accomplish this?

What type of work would you like to be doing 5-10 years from now? What do you need to do now to bring this to reality?

What additional career goals would you like to achieve? How will you go about accomplishing this?

Goal 1:

Goal Category (personal, academic, etc):

Type of Goal (short, mid-range, long-term):

How is it:

Specific:

Measurable:

Attainable:

Realistic:

Timely:

Relatable:

Goal 2:

Goal Category (personal, academic, etc):

Type of Goal (short, mid-range, long-term):

How is it:

Specific:

Measurable:

Attainable:

Realistic:

Timely:

Relatable:

Goal 3:

Goal Category (personal, academic, etc):

Type of Goal (short, mid-range, long-term):

How is it:

Specific:

Measurable:

Attainable:

Realistic:

Timely:

Relatable:

Goal 4:

Goal Category (personal, academic, etc):

Type of Goal (short, mid-range, long-term):

How is it:

Specific:

Measurable:

Attainable:

Realistic:

Timely:

Relatable:

Goal 5:

Goal Category (personal, academic, etc):

Type of Goal (short, mid-range, long-term):

How is it:

Specific:

Measurable:

Attainable:

Realistic:

Timely:

Relatable:

Select your Top 3 Goals for each goal type and list them below

Short-Term	Mid-Range	Long-Range
1 _____	1 _____	1 _____
2 _____	2 _____	2 _____
3 _____	3 _____	3 _____

List potential obstacles, risks and/or challenges you could encounter that will prevent you from accomplishing these goals.

1.

2.

3.

4.

5.

6.

What tactics or strategies will you employ to mitigate and/or minimize the impact of these potential obstacles from delaying your progress?

-
-
-
-
-
-

What investments/sacrifices will you need to make in order to accomplish your goals. (time, money, club involvement, hanging with friends, etc.)

1.

2.

3.

What training, skills, education, etc. will you need for your toolkit in order to accomplish your goals, mission and/or vision? Include how you will accomplish it.

1.

2.

3.

Identify people, groups or organizations whose help and cooperation you will need to achieve this goal. What role will they play.

-
-
-
-
-
-

Name people who can serve as your Accountability Team and support you along this journey.

1.

2.

3.

4.

5.

Life/Growth Planning

Mission

_____

_____

_____

_____

Vision

_____

_____

_____

_____

Values Statement

_____

_____

_____

_____

Based on your gifts, skills and talents, who do they align with your mission and vision? How does your desired career path fit in and support these factors? (There should be an alignment – Complete a Career Assessment)

What are the Top 3 to 5 Careers you could pursue that aligns with your mission and vision?

1.

2.

3.

4.

5.

Let's research your desired career path to see what the job forecast looks like and see if it is a growing, declining or stagnant career. Use this to make the best career selection decision.

Occupational Research Questionnaire:

Identify your desired career field of study. Then research and capture key data points about the career from the Bureau of Labor and Statistics (BLS) website, Onet Online (onetonline.org).

Occupation:

Educational Requirement(s):

Job Forecast:

Typical Job Responsibility:

Typical Working Conditions:

Related/Similar Careers:

Salary Range:

Work Schedule:

Travel Requirements:

Training/Licensing Requirements:

States with the Best Job Opportunities:

How has this professions faired in occupation?

Academics

How strong is your GPA (not necessarily how high)? It's all about the rigor represented on your transcript from 9th -11th grade. What you do or don't do in Middle School to initiate a rigorous approach will impact your level of access to rigorous courses in 9th grade.

Does Your Transcript Show Rigor?

Colleges are looking for students who didn't shy away from taking courses that represent "rigor" and don't fall under "basic" high school courses. Rigorous courses typically carry more weight for the grade and results in a weighted GPA.

Over your 4 years in HS, your transcript should have a combination of the following courses. The more selective the college you are targeting is, the more advanced classes you must have on your transcript. That means 9th Grade must have a series of these classes. For this to happen, your Middle School transcript must have rigor as well.

Four years of English

Four years of Mathematics — including Algebra 1 and 2, Geometry, and preferably at least one other advanced Mathematics course such as Trigonometry, Pre-Calculus, Calculus, or Statistics

Two years of a World Language

Three years of Laboratory Science such as Biology, Chemistry, and Physics

Three years of Social Studies

Here are examples of courses that represent rigor.

Algebra I & II	Pre-Calc & Calculus	Biology	Chemistry
Physics	Trigonometry	Statistics	
Honors	AP Courses	IB Courses	Dual Enrollment Courses

How many "rigorous" courses have you taken? _____

How many do you need for the school you are targeting? _____

Test scores

Although there's a push to diminish the value of the college admissions exam, it is still a factor. So, the higher the score the more opportunities you can qualify for. The goal is Early and Often! Don't wait until the last minute to start.

Test Preparation: Taking The Psat, Sat and Act

COLLEGE EXAMINATION TIMELINE

8th grade/ freshman

Build Vocabulary- vocabulary exercises word games and ACT/SAT prep books

Enroll in AP (advanced placement) and IB (international baccalaureate) courses

sophomore

summer (before)

Build Vocabulary- vocabulary exercises word games and ACT/SAT prep books

Understand test taking strategies

ACT/SAT test preparation classes

PSAT in october for practice PLAN (preliminary ACT)

fall

Build Vocabulary II- word origins, synonyms, antonyms

Enroll in AP (advanced placement) and IB (international baccalaureate) courses

spring

Understand test taking strategies

ACT/SAT test preparation classes

Enroll in AP (advanced placement) and IB (international baccalaureate) courses

junior

summer (before)

Vocabulary Exercises

ACT/SAT test preparation classes

fall

PSAT- take actual exam to qualify for National Merit Scholarship

Enroll in AP (advanced placement) and IB (international baccalaureate) courses

Take SAT
Take ACT

spring

Take AP/IB subject area tests

Take SAT subject area tests

Senior

fall

Take SAT, if needed

Take ACT, if needed

Take SAT subject area test, if needed

spring

Register and take AP subject area tests

Register and take IB subject area tests

Enroll in AP (advanced placement) and IB (international baccalaureate) courses

My Target ACT/SAT Scores

Your goal here is to perform either at the average level or above. So, you will review the stats in these areas for the schools you are targeting and establish them as your goal/target GPA and ACT/SAT Test Score.

University/ College	Average GPA for Incoming Freshmen	Average SAT for Incoming Freshmen	Average ACT for Incoming Freshmen	Your GPA (weighted & unweighted)	Your Highest ACT/SAT

College Admissions

There are many facets to understand regarding the college admissions process. You must target the "right" schools, but that means you must gather the appropriate details and plan accordingly.

10 Tips
for Selecting the "Right" School

This checklist gives you an overview of the key things you should do for selecting the right school. Asking the right questions and identifying the right information will enable you to narrow down your school choices, make the right selection that best fits you.

1

Select the type of school you want to attend.

First you have public and private schools. Then you have community, technical, trade, Ivy League, State Schools/Public Institutions and Historically Black Colleges and Universities. Each school has its own characteristics, qualities, assets and uniqueness. See which ones will provide the right atmosphere and support for learning.

2

Select the size of school you want to attend.

Colleges come in all shapes and sizes. So, you must choose a school that works best for you. Don't just get caught up in the name and its notoriety, know if the school is conducive for your learning and success.

Do you perform well in a class of 100 or a more intimate setting of 30 or less students?

3

Identify the state you want to be in.

This may be a "no-brainer," but it's a question worth asking. Some colleges have the luxury of being placed in major metropolitan areas, where others are in small rural towns or somewhere in between. Depending on your preferences, this will make a difference in

your school selection. Does being close to major shopping areas, airports and the social scene mean anything to you or not?

4

Does the school have an accredited program in the area you plan to study?

It's important to check the school's accreditation rating to ensure the program you are pursuing is nationally accredited. Accredited programs are what companies look for when recruiting college graduates.

5
Create a list of amenities you "must" have and "would like" to have in a school.
As stated, each school has its own uniqueness and offerings. Is there a particular club/ organization you want to be a part of? Or is sports big in your book? Perhaps you want nice on-campus living. Whatever it is, make your lists and compare it to your school choices.

6
Research the schools giving/financial aid award history.
Believe it or not, this information is out there. Some schools cover 100% of need, while others cover only 65% and/or build their financial aid packages with various loans. This is why it's important to see how the schools on your list rank. You can also target schools committed to minimizing the student loan debt, but know they are competitive to get in. So, you must be ready. To see these list of schools, check out The Education Trust Access to Success. The Access to Success Initiative is a project of the National Association of System Heads (NASH) and The Education Trust. A2S works with 22 public higher education systems that have pledged to cut the college-going and graduation
gaps for low-income and minority students in half by 2015. Together, these institutions serve more than 3.5 million students.

7
Research the schools employability statistics for their graduates.
The purpose of getting a degree is so you can pursue your career dreams. What good is a degree from a school who is negligent in building and forming the right relationships with industry partners to facilitate employment opportunities for their graduates? Do your due diligence and check out the schools on your list.

8
Schedule Campus Visits
The purpose of seeing a campus live and in the flesh is so you can truly assess if it's a good fit or not. You must get a feel for the culture of the campus, it's surrounding environment, dorm living, activities, etc. If there is something that make you feel uncomfortable during your visit, take heed and note of it because it may be a factor in your decision process.

9
Determine the average length of time students graduate
Are the schools on your list graduating students before, after or at the US average of 5 1/2 years? Because of limited aid, increasing tuition and large student loan debt, some schools are promising graduation in 4 years or the additional tuition will be free. Weigh all of your options.

10
What partnerships does the school have with corporations and organizations to enhance learning?
Partnerships with corporations and organizations foster funding opportunities for new programs, research, work-study opportunities, scholarships and job s.

6 College Admissions Secrets

The "Hook" Advantage:

having a "hook" means you have an advantage with your admissions application. Falling under a "hook" gives you a better position compared to other applicants, as it will improve your odds of being admitted. Top tier universities (Ivy's and more) use a hook in their admissions process. You may be wondering what a hook is. Here are some of the main hooks:
- Alumni connections or your legacy connection (mother, father and possibly grandparent) can open the door.
- Underrepresented ethnicities (African-Americans, American Indian/Native American, Mexican-American/Latino, Asian American/Pacific Islander, multi-racial or bi-racial, etc.)
- Athletes, especially top-performing recruited athletes can receive some favor during the admissions process.
- High Profile or VIP affiliations

The Early Bird Gets the Worm - Early Decision:

colleges have a greater interest in students fully committed to attending their university, as it helps them with their forecasting and planning efforts. Early decision implies the student is beyond interested in the university, and dedicated to pursuing the process of admissions. Because this approach requires a commitment, the applicant pool is much smaller than other admissions options. If a student is confident in their school selection, they should pursue this route for admissions. Not only does it increase a student's chance for admittance, but also for money.

Image is Everything - Brand "You":

there aren't enough conversation about image and branding when it comes to students. As students begin the admissions process with schools, the research begins on the student where information is captured and filed.

Schools are interested in students who will represent them well and carry on their legacy in a positive and influential way post-graduation. If your communications with the school lacks professionalism, respect, etiquette; or social media profile showcases bad behavior, irresponsibility, etc. you are considered a liability and high risk factor. Copies, screenshots, and print-outs from Facebook, Twitter, LinkedIn, YouTube, websites, etc. are taken and captured in your file. You should always Google yourself to see what type of images, commentary and posts are associated with your name. This can make or break their decision to admit you. What brand/image do you want your perspective college(s) to perceive of you? Ask yourself this question every time you interact with a college rep, your teachers, post something on the internet, etc. To take it a step further, keep this in mind when you create your email address, select your phone ringtone and voicemail.

Take the Direct Approach, Face to Face is Always Better:

establishing, cultivating and managing relationships is always a good thing. The answer to your problem is always a person. For this reason, you don't want to settle for phone and email conversations only, a live and in-person visit can be worthwhile. Go and establish a personal contact and nurture it. If the school conducts interviews and give you the option for face-to-face vs. phone, go with the face-to-face option. There are some things you can only convey in person and that can contribute to your selling point.

Maximize Your Family's Socioeconomic Background:

don't be embarrassed if you didn't come from money, don't live in the right zip code or are the first in your family to go to college. Know that this is okay, it is your truth for you to own because it can work out in your favor. Many colleges capture this information so they can track the number of "first generation" and/or "low-income" students attend their university. Often times, there is money allocated for students in these areas. So, don't hide it, but highlight it! It's your truth, own it!

Know What's in Your File:

just like a professional in the workforce, you should know what Is in your personnel file, or school file in your case. Colleges will request your college profile from your high school and you should familiarize yourself with what they will be receiving. Check it to ensure it is accurate, especially your transcript. Are your receiving credit for all the courses you've completed, are your grades correct, etc. Your college profile entails class rank, offerings at the school, grading and ranking policy, school demographics, test scores, GPA (weighted and unweighted), to possibly a few more traits. Be informed.

You can do all of these things right, but if you don't submit a strong application, it may be meaningless. So, it's important for students to not lose sight of the foundational elements, the college application. Regardless of how students submit their college application, directly to the school or via the common application, the college essay must be strong and of excellence. This is the time where students are given permission to brag on themselves. Focus on marketing your talents, skills, leadership, community service, and academic accomplishments. Showcase it in a way that you can demonstrate how you will be an asset to the university and impact the school in a positive way.

Centralized College Application Portals

The Common Application

Five Hundred plus (500+) colleges and universities have agreed to accept a generic application called the Common Application. This allows students to submit applications to many schools using the same forms. The Common Application is only available online at www.commonapp.org. Note that, in many cases, the school will accept the Common Application but will also require additional information given by way of a supplement to the application (also found on the Common Application website). Check the school's website for the most current information regarding any necessary supplements.

The Common Black Application

The Common Black College Application allows students to apply to any number of 57 HBCUs at the same time for only $20. On March 17, 2015 the California Community Colleges and nine Historically Black Colleges and Universities, established an agreement that will allow college students who complete certain academic requirements guaranteed transfer to a participating HBCU. Available at http://commonblackcollegeapp.com/

The Universal College Application

The Universal College Application is accepted by more than 30 colleges and universities. You can register as an applicant in order to start applying.

The Coalition Application

The Coalition Application is accepted by more than 90 institutions. The platform includes "The Locker," a private space for you to collect and organize materials throughout high school that you might want to share with colleges and universities.

Types of Admissions

Early Decision (ED) Applications

An Early Decision agreement means that if a student is admitted, the student will attend that school (in many cases, regardless of the amount of financial aid offered by the school). Most colleges have three options for Early Decision applicants: they will admit you, defer your admission for further review, or deny your admission. Some colleges may not "defer" from the Early Decision applicant pool, meaning that you will be either admitted or denied (check with the individual college if their stated policy is unclear). Submitting an Early Decision application is a commitment to attend that school if you are accepted; therefore, you may only submit one Early Decision Application, and, if accepted, you must withdraw any applications submitted to other schools. It is the student's responsibility to know the ED applications rules for the school to which they are applying. Some colleges accept a larger number of students from their early decision pool than their regular decision pool. However, a student should only use this method of application if (1) the applicant is absolutely certain that the college is their first choice, and (2) the applicant is absolutely certain that they can afford the cost of attendance (advance conversations with the college's financial aid office may be very helpful in making this determination).

Early Action (EA) Applications

Early Action plans allow the student to receive the admission decision from a college or university early, but also allows the student to apply to other schools and to wait to make a final decision until May 1. Under this application program, colleges may admit you, defer your admission for further review, or deny your admission. In a few instances, schools accepting EA applications will restrict students from applying to other schools by EA or ED (this sometimes referred to a "Restricted Early Action"). It is the student's responsibility to know the rules of EA applications for the specific school(s) to which they are applying.

Rolling Admissions

Colleges that use Rolling Admissions evaluate and accept or deny students' admission several weeks following the receipt of their applications. Students wishing to attend a school with a rolling admission plan should generally submit applications early in the Fall in order to ensure that a space will still be available for them to attend this institution. Please note that these schools frequently publish deadlines for application in the late spring, but their freshman classes can be full well before that date. Complete the appropriate online application. Take your time to complete it to the best of your ability. Do not 'submit' until you have completed the essays and thoroughly reviewed all the information. You can save and return to it later to continue working on it.

Choosing A
College/ University/ Vocational School

Based on the career profession you plan to pursue, what type of educational institution does it require?

☐ Trade School ☐ Community College ☐ 4-Year College

List your Top 5 Colleges/ Universities

Schools	State

List the Top 5 Schools for Your Chosen Career Field of Study

School Questionnaire

Take each school and gather more details to narrow down and select the best school(s) for you to pursue.

College/University:

Location:

Major: Student Population:

Accrediting Agency: School Ranking:

Are SAT/ACT Tests Required: Avg. SAT/ ACT Scored:

Teacher to Student Ratio:

Application Deadline(s):   Essay Required:

Application Fee: Freshmen retention rate:

Do graduate students teach freshmen?

What percentage of students graduate in 4 years?

What percentage of students graduate in 5 years?

What does a typical freshman schedule look like?

School location (city, urban or rural) area?

Distance from airport:

What social offerings are available (sororities, fraternities, sports, etc.)?

Can Freshmen have cars?   Is there a bus system?

How Freshmen are housed—Coed Dorms, Single-Sex dorms, Honor Dorms, or Freshmen Dorms?

What is supplied in the dorms (appliances, washer & dryer, desk, etc.)?

How are roommates assigned?

Is this a state supported school?

Does the school waive Out-Of-State fees?   Requirements

How much are out-of-state fees?   ROTC Programs

What is the Net Price to attend?

What percentage of need is met?

How do they fund (merit, need or combination)

What corporations partner with the school

What is the make-up of financial aid packages (% of Free Money (scholarships, grants, etc) vs. Non-Free Money (Student and Parent Loans))?

Does the state have a reciprocity agreement, whereby out-of-state fees may be waived?

Tuition Costs:

Room & Board:

Miscellaneous Fees:

What are the meal options?

College Visit Profile

COLLEGE/UNIVERSITY:

EMAIL:

LOCATION:

COUNSELOR:

COLLEGE ADMISSIONS REP:

PHONE:

PHONE:

EMAIL:

EMAIL:

COLLEGE DEAN:

FINANCIAL AID OFFICER:

PHONE:

PHONE:

EMAIL:

Observations

FIRST IMPRESSIONS

THE DORMS

THE DINING HALLS

TOWN/CITY AND SURROUNDING AREA OF THE CAMPUS

Parent's Thoughts

TOP 3 LIKES

TOP 3 DISLIKES

College Comparison Sheet

GENERL INFORMATION	SCHOOL 1	SCHOOL 2	SCHOOL 3
Location			
Rank information			
Web address			
Size			
Colleges and schools			
other			
APPLYING			
Admissions address			
Admissions telephone			
Contact person			
Application fee			
Date application due			
Send transcripts to			
Date application mailed			

Accepted?

Accept or decline by date

Other

REQUIREMENTS

SAT minimum score

ACT minimum score

Other standardized tests

Grades

Advanced placement
(AP) scores?

International
Baccalaureate (IB) credit?

Essay requirements

Personal document
requirements

Resume requirements

Community/ volunteer
work

Other

FINANCES

	SCHOOL 1	SCHOOL 2	SCHOOL 3
Yearly tuition (non-resident)			
Out of State Fees			
Books/supplies			
Room and board			
Transportation			
Medical			
Personal			
Estimated total			
Financial Aid Pell Grant			
Financial Aid - Student Loan			
Scholarship info			
Student employment info			
Financial aid office location			
Financial aid office telephone			
Other			

NON-ACADEMIC STUDENT ACTIVITIES	SCHOOL 1	SCHOOL 2	SCHOOL 3
Club sports rm interested in			
Greek system?			
Other			

CAMPUS VISITS

	SCHOOL 1	SCHOOL 2	SCHOOL 3
When			
Contact person			
Contacts phone number/e-mail			
Accommodations - Dormatory, Cafeteria, etc			
Campus Appearance			
College/Department Ammenities			

SURROUNDING AREA

	SCHOOL 1	SCHOOL 2	SCHOOL 3
City, state			
Accessiblity to Mall, Stores, Shopping (miles)			
Accessibility to Airport			
Distance from Home (hours and miles)			
Average Plane Ticket			

Population

Median income

Average rental cost
(2 bedroom)

Top 5 county employers

Average weather

NOTES

MANAGEMENT PROCESS

Answer

College: _____

Deadline: _____

Q1 Application

Date Submitted: _____

Date of Acceptance: _____

Q2 Transcripts

Date of Request: _____

Confirmation Date: _____

Q3 Standardized Tests

ACT

Date of Registration: _____

Test Taken (Date): _____

Scores: _____

SAT

Date of Registration: _____

Test Taken (Date): _____

Scores: _____

SAT Subject Tests

Date of Registration: _____

Test Taken (Date): _____

Scores: _____

Q4 Test Scores Requested To Be Sent To University

ACT: _____

SAT: _____

SAT Subject Test: _____

AP/IB: _____

Q5 | Letters of Recommendation

Number Needed:
Requested From:
]]Requested Date:
Date Received:
Thank You Note Sent:

Essays

Q6

How Many?
Brainstorming Session:
Rough Draft:
Second Draft:
Final Draft:
Proofread by Someone:

Q7 | Financial Aid

Deadline
College/University Specific Forms:
Information Gathered:
Copies Made:
Forms Submitted:

FAFSA

Information Gathered:
Copies Made:
Forms Submitted:
SAR Report

Answer

Q8 ## Verification

Call Admissions Rep and Verify
Receipt of Application:
Call Financial Aid Office and Verify
Receipt of Application:
Admissions Response Received:
Admission Acceptance Letter
Returned:
Housing Deposit Sent:
Scholarship/ Financial Aid
Acceptance Returned:
Declining Acceptance Letter Sent:
Declining Financial Aid Sent:
Thank-You Letter Sent for
Scholarship:

Q9 ## Final Steps

Freshmen Orientation Scheduled:
Enroll in Classes:
Contacted Roommate:
Scheduled Campus Move Date &
Travel Arrangements:
School's Suggested Reading List:
Date Reading List Completed:

ESSAY BRAINSTORMING PROCESS

Brainstorming is the beginning process to writing an essay. Brainstorming will help you generate ideas, think about the essay and give you a new context in which to view the subject matter. All thoughts are allowed when you are brainstorming. No idea is a bad idea, so write down everything that comes to mind concerning the topic. If you need further inspiration to get your creative juices flowing, ask yourself "why" to each point you write down.

_____

_____

_____

_____   Role Models

_____

_____

                              _____

                              _____

Political   _____
situations that
make you angry   _____

                              _____

                              _____

_____
_____
_____
_____
_____

Political events or
ethical issues that
have inspired you
to change your
own life, behavior,
or the world
around you

Characters from
fiction that you'd
like to meet

_____
_____
_____
_____
_____

_____
_____
_____
_____

Humiliating
experiences
you've had. How
have they
impacted you

Accomplishments
you've achieved.
Why are they
important to you

_____
_____
_____
_____
_____

Negative
misconceptions
people have
about you

_____
_____
_____
_____
_____

The best
decision(s) you
have made in
your life

_____
_____
_____
_____
_____

The worst
decision(s) you
have made in
your life

_____
_____
_____
_____
_____

How have you
changed in the
past three years

_____
_____
_____
_____
_____

PREWRITING
INTERVIEWS

Sometimes it's a challenge to identify characteristics about ourselves along with tooting our own horns. That is why you seek the advice and input of friends, relatives, teachers, etc. Here are some questions you can ask about two to three people to give you more details to include in your essay and use for their college interview.

WHAT ARE THREE ADJECTIVES THAT DESCRIBE ME?

First Person

Second Person

Third Person

WHEN WERE YOU MOST PROUD OF ME?

First Person

Second Person

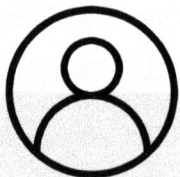

Third Person

WHAT DO YOU THINK ARE MY THREE GREATEST STRENGTHS?

First Person

Second Person

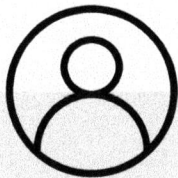

Third Person

WHAT DO YOU THINK ARE MY THREE AREAS OF WEAKNESS?

First Person

Second Person

Third Person

ADMISSIONS INTERVIEW
questions

Anticipating what you will be asked is a good way to prepare for an interview. Going through this process will also prevent the use of filler words such as: urns, ers, and I don't know. Practice answering these questions with family members and friends.

✓ WHY DO YOU WANT TO GO HERE?

✓ WHAT DO YOU WANT TO MAJOR IN?

✓ WHAT ARE YOUR INTERESTS?

✓ WHAT BOOKS HAVE HAD AN IMPACT ON YOU?

✓ WHAT ARE YOUR STRENGTHS AND WEAKNESSES?

✓ WHAT ARE YOUR PLANS AFTER COLLEGE?

✓ HOW INVOLVED HAVE YOU BEEN IN YOUR COMMUNITY?

✓ WHAT IS THE MISSION OF YOUR SCHOOL'S PRESIDENT?

✓ HOW HAS ENROLLMENT CHANGED THE PAST 5 YEARS?

✓ HOW AND WHERE DO STUDENTS FALL SHORT?

✓ WHAT KIND OF STUDENTS DO YOU LIKE TO ATTRACT?

✓ WHAT IS THE BEST WAY TO SUCCEED AT YOUR UNIVERSITY?

✓ WHAT IS THE BEST WAY TO PREPARE FOR YOUR UNIVERSITY?

✓ WHAT DO YOU WANT STUDENTS TO KNOW ABOUT YOUR UNIVERSITY?

✓ HOW MANY STUDENTS APPLY EACH YEAR? HOW MANY ARE ACCEPTED?

✓ WHAT ARE THE AVERAGE GPA AND AVERAGE ACT ASSESSMENT OR SAT I SCORE(S) FOR THOSE ACCEPTED?

✓ HOW MANY STUDENTS IN LAST YEAR'S FRESHMAN CLASS RETURNED FOR THEIR SOPHOMORE YEAR?

✓ WHAT IS THE SCHOOL'S PROCEDURE FOR CREDIT FOR ADVANCED PLACEMENT HIGH SCHOOL COURSES?

✓ AS A FRESHMAN, WILL I BE TAUGHT BY PROFESSORS OR TEACHING ASSISTANTS?

✓ HOW MANY STUDENTS ARE THERE PER TEACHER?

✓ WHEN IS IT NECESSARY TO DECLARE A MAJOR?

✓ IS IT POSSIBLE TO HAVE A DOUBLE MAJOR OR TO DECLARE A MAJOR AND A MINOR?

✓ WHAT ARE THE REQUIREMENTS FOR THE MAJOR IN WHICH I AM INTERESTED?

✓ HOW DOES THE ADVISING SYSTEM WORK?

✓ DOES THIS COLLEGE OFFER STUDY ABROAD, COOPERATIVE PROGRAMS, OR ACADEMIC HONORS PROGRAMS?

- ✓ WHAT IS THE LIKELIHOOD, DUE TO OVERCROWDING, OF GETTING CLOSED OUT OF THE COURSES I NEED?
- ✓ WHAT TECHNOLOGY IS AVAILABLE, AND WHAT ARE ANY ASSOCIATED FEES?
- ✓ HOW WELL EQUIPPED ARE THE LIBRARIES AND LABORATORIES?
- ✓ ARE INTERNSHIPS AVAILABLE?
- ✓ HOW EFFECTIVE IS THE JOB PLACEMENT SERVICE OF THE SCHOOL?

- ✓ WHAT IS THE AVERAGE CLASS SIZE IN MY AREA OF INTEREST?
- ✓ HAVE ANY PROFESSORS IN MY AREA OF INTEREST RECENTLY WON ANY HONORS OR AWARDS?
- ✓ WHAT TEACHING METHODS ARE USED IN MY AREA OF INTEREST (LECTURE, GROUP DISCUSSION, FIELDWORK)?
- ✓ HOW MANY STUDENTS GRADUATE IN FOUR YEARS IN MY AREA OF INTEREST?
- ✓ WHAT ARE THE SPECIAL REQUIREMENTS FOR GRADUATION IN MY AREA OF INTEREST?

- ✓ WHAT IS THE STUDENT BODY LIKE? AGE? SEX? RACE? GEOGRAPHIC ORIGIN?
- ✓ WHAT PERCENTAGE OF STUDENTS LIVE IN DORMITORIES? OFF-CAMPUS HOUSING?
- ✓ WHAT PERCENTAGE OF STUDENTS GO HOME FOR THE WEEKEND?
- ✓ WHAT ARE SOME OF THE REGULATIONS THAT APPLY TO LIVING IN A DORMITORY?
- ✓ WHAT ARE THE SECURITY PRECAUTIONS TAKEN ON CAMPUS AND IN THE DORMS?

- ✓ IS THE SURROUNDING COMMUNITY SAFE?
- ✓ ARE THERE PROBLEMS WITH DRUG AND ALCOHOL ABUSE ON CAMPUS?
- ✓ DO FACULTY MEMBERS AND STUDENTS MIX ON AN INFORMAL BASIS?
- ✓ HOW IMPORTANT ARE THE ARTS TO STUDENT LIFE?
- ✓ WHAT FACILITIES ARE AVAILABLE FOR CULTURAL EVENTS?

- ✓ HOW IMPORTANT ARE SPORTS TO STUDENT LIFE?
- ✓ WHAT FACILITIES ARE AVAILABLE FOR SPORTING EVENTS?
- ✓ WHAT PERCENTAGE OF THE STUDENT BODY BELONGS TO A SORORITY/ FRATERNITY?
- ✓ WHAT IS THE RELATIONSHIP BETWEEN THOSE WHO BELONG TO THE GREEK SYSTEM AND THOSE WHO DON'T?
- ✓ ARE STUDENTS INVOLVED IN THE DECISION-MAKING PROCESS AT THE COLLEGE? DO THEY SIT ON MAJOR COMMITTEES?

- ✓ IN WHAT OTHER ACTIVITIES CAN STUDENTS GET INVOLVED?
- ✓ WHAT PERCENTAGE OF STUDENTS RECEIVE FINANCIAL AID BASED ON NEED?
- ✓ WHAT PERCENTAGE OF STUDENTS RECEIVE SCHOLARSHIPS BASED ON ACADEMIC ABILITY?
- ✓ WHAT PERCENTAGE OF A TYPICAL FINANCIAL AID OFFER IS IN THE FORM OF A LOAN?
- ✓ IF MY FAMILY DEMONSTRATES FINANCIAL NEED ON THE FAF SA (AND PROFILE®, IF APPLICABLE), WHAT PERCENTAGE OF THE ESTABLISHED NEED IS GENERALLY AWARDED?

- ✓ HOW MUCH DID THE COLLEGE INCREASE THE COST OF ROOM, BOARD, TUITION, AND FEES FROM LAST YEAR?
- ✓ DO OPPORTUNITIES FOR FINANCIAL AID, SCHOLARSHIPS, OR WORK-STUDY INCREASE EACH YEAR?
- ✓ WHEN IS THE ADMISSION APPLICATION DEADLINE?
- ✓ WHEN IS THE FINANCIAL AID APPLICATION DEADLINE?
- ✓ WHEN WILL I BE NOTIFIED OF THE ADMISSION DECISION?

College Funding

College funding involves scholarships, financial aid, government funding, military, student loans, etc. Our focus here is on understanding some basics regarding financial aid and positioning yourself for scholarship opportunities.

FINANCIAL AID

Q1 What type of college are you targeting?

_____
_____
_____

Q2 What funding options can your child start doing to contribute to their college process?

_____
_____
_____

Q3 Is your child performing at the Top 25% of their class?

_____
_____

Q4 Is your child's test scores (ACT/SAT/PSAT) in the top 25%? If not, where are they?

_____
_____

Q5 What is your estimated EFC?

_____
_____

Q6 What year will you be required to submit the FAFSA? What tax year will be used to determine your child's financial aid?

_____
_____
_____

Q7 What assets do you possess that can reduce your need?

_____
_____
_____

Q8 Identify and research 4 schools you are targeting and complete the table below to determine how much money you should aim to acquire in private scholarships.

SCHOOLS (Enter School Name at Top of Heading)

COA				
FAMILY CONTRIBUTION (EFC)				
FINANCIAL NEED				
%NEED MET OF SCHOOL				
AMOUNT I NEED IN PRIVATE SCHOLARSHIPS (Mulitiply % Need Met x Financial Need)				

Q9 Based on your EFC and total Need Amount, what is your Financial Aid goal(s)?

_____

_____

_____

_____

_____

_____

_____

_____

Q10 What gaps and/or assets do you have you need to improve and/or can build upon?

_____

_____

_____

_____

_____

_____

_____

_____

Q11   Who do you need to talk to about being on your team?

_____

_____

_____

_____

_____

_____

Q12   Based on the information outlined above, what do you need to start doing and/or do more of to meet your financial aid goals? Your strategy?

_____

_____

_____

_____

_____

_____

Q13   What are the things your child can do to contribute to this process? Identify actions they need to take and assign a deadline.

_____

_____

_____

_____

_____

Q14   What do you currently have that will fund college tuition?

_____

_____

_____

_____

_____

Q15   Do you meet the income threshold of "need based" scholarships? (research need based scholarships for income brackets) Does your child have strong academics to meet "merit" scholarship requirements? (research merit based scholarships for varying requirements) If not, can you do anything differently to qualify for either?

_____
_____
_____
_____
_____

Q16   Are there specialty areas your child can gain funding in? Is your child competitive enough to get funded? Are they disciplined enough to meet the scholarship requirements and time management?

_____
_____
_____
_____
_____

Q17   What are your next steps and corresponding timeframe and frequency?

_____
_____
_____
_____
_____

Additional Notes

_____
_____
_____
_____

Scholarship Application Tracking Sheet

Translate this form into an electronic document so you can track your scholarships applications and their corresponding deadlines. They key to this process is planning, time management and managing deadlines.

Scholarship	Award Amount	Reduired Area(s) Study	Created Application Checklist	Deadline	Application Date	Outcome

SCHOLARSHIP
PROFILE
SHEET

SCHOLARSHIP NAME:

_____

DEADLINE:

_____

SCHOLARSHIP SOURCE/SPONSOR:

SCHOLARSHIP AMOUNT:

WEB ADDRESS:

IS IT RENEWABLE:

CONTACT INFO:

AREA(S) OF STUDY REQUIREMENT:

_____

REQUIREMENTS:

NUMBER OF

RECOMMENDATIONS REQUIRED:

_____

RECOMMENDATIONS

REQUESTED BY:

_____

_____

_____

_____

_____

AWARD NOTIFICATION DATE:

GENERAL NOTES:

SUBMITTAL CHECKLIST:

	Completed Application
	Completed & Proofed Essay
	Recommendation Letters
	Transcripts
	Test Scores
	Community Service Profile

Financial Budget Sheet

College is expensive, but many fail to plan. This is one of many budgetary tools you can use to plan for everything college.

Complete the cells below or create an electronic version of it. This tool will enable you to gain insight about what your financial gap could be and how hard you need to work to earn scholarships.

	Contribution	Per Semester	Year	Gap
Job				
Parents/Family				
Loans				
Scholarships				
Financial Aid				
TOTAL				

	Expense	Per Semester	Year	Gap
 Tuition				
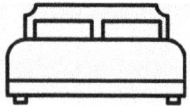 Room& Board				
 Books				
Meals				
Phone				
Internet				
 Car				
 Rent (off Campus)				
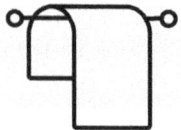 Utilities (off Campus)				
 Travel Home				
Miscellaneous				
TOTAL				

Monthly *Income*

Item	Amount
Estimated monthly net income	
Financial aid award(s)	
Other income	
Total	

Monthly *Expenses*

Item	Amount
Rent	
Utilities	
Cell phone	
Groceries	
Auto expenses	
Student loans	
Other loans	
Credit cards	
Insurance	
Laundry	
Hair cuts	
Medical expenses	
Entertainment	
Miscellaneous	
Total	

Student Name

Guardian

Schooll/College

Semester *Expenses*

Item	Amount
Tuition	
Lab fees	
Other fees	
Books	
Deposits	
Transportation	
Total	

Discretionary *Income*

Item	Amount
Monthly Income	
Monthly expenses	
Semester expenses	
Difference	

Leadership

How have you engaged in non-academic activities and demonstrated strong leadership skills? That's what this section is about. Highlight your extra-curricular activities and the impact associated with your engagement.

College and Scholarship funders are not looking for students who blend in with the crowd. Not only is it critical for you to build a "fundable" profile, but you must know how to market your unique abilities so you attract "fundable" opportunities.

What leadership roles have you held from 9th-11th grade (give organization, grade when involved and role)?

Describe the impact or difference you made as a member of these organizations. What value did you add? How did you make things better?

Create your Leadership Impact statement. (Summarize who you are as a leader, what you've done, and the difference you've made)

Academics

What does your academic profile look like? (Summarize what honor classes you've taken, IB/AP courses, college or correspondent classes from your 9th-11th grade)

Summarize your academic profile. (GPA - weighted and unweighted, class rank and academic accolades)

Community Service

What community service have you been involved in from 9th-11th grade (give organization, grade when involved, role and hours served)?

Describe the impact or difference you made as a result of your participation in the activity and/or organization. What value did you add? How did you make things better? What was the result of the community service activity?

Test Scores

What are your ACT and/or SAT test scores?

Awards & Recognition

List all of the awards, honors and recognitions you've received from 9th-11th grade.

Additional Extra-curricular Activities

List other extra-curricular activities you participated in from 9th-11th grade.

What unique characteristics or traits do you have? What makes you stand out from other students? What activities have you participated in most students your age haven't?

Social Media Review

Google your name, were there any negative or unfavorable results?

Examine all of your social media profiles. Do you have any negative pictures or posts that could cause you to be viewed unfavorably (sexually related, drugs, alcohol, bullying, etc.)?

Unique Selling Position (USP) Statement

Create your personal USP impact statement in less than 50 words.

Now that you've captured information on what makes you unique and stand out, it's time to share and market yourself. Below are a couple of places to start making your unique talents visible to key decision-makers in the college admissions and funding world.

Create a LinkedIn account and include this information

Create a Student Resume

Create profiles on scholarship search engines and platforms (Ex. Scholly App, Raise.me, Cappex, etc.)

Community Service

A strong quality of a "Leader" is their ability to be selfless. Schools and scholarship organizations want Leaders who care about others and have a desire to give back. So, it's like this: What Have You Done For Others or When Was the Last Time You Did Something Meaningful for Somebody Else; not, What Can I Get Out of This for Myself.

Like Leadership, everyone is looking for selfless leaders looking to make a difference. So, you want to capture your level of impact in service opportunities you engaged in that did not yield a grade. You can't count "volunteer" hours if it was part of a grade or graduation requirements. Real leaders go above and beyond that.

Community Service Source	Amount of Hours Volunteered	Dates	Impact and/ or Result

Tip Sheet: List your Awards & Accolades

The college admissions and scholarship process is not the time to be bashful. Track and promote your accolades and recognition.

Recognition/Award	School Year	Award Details

Tip Sheet: Letters of Recommendations

For the college admissions and scholarship process, you will need letters of recommendation to fulfill application requirements. The goal is to target people who really know you and can provide specific details in a letter that makes you attractive to the reader and a magnet for the opportunity you are applying for.

Person	Role	Yrs Knowing Them

FAQs

How soon should I start applying for scholarships?

It's never too early to start. There are scholarships available as early as Kindergarten

Is there a time when I can stop applying for scholarships?

No. Although the availability of scholarships are less once you become a college student, it doesn't mean you stop applying. You only stop when you are finish with school.

We make too much money; can we still qualify for scholarships?

Yes. There are many scholarships based on merit (academics), community service, social issues, hobbies, talents, specialty crafts, health factors, disabilities, etc. In essence, there is a scholarship for literally every and anything (ADD, Being Left-handed, Flat Footed, Creating a Greeting Card or a PSA Video, etc.)

What's the difference between Test Optional and Test Blind?

Test Optional schools don't require the ACT/SAT for admissions, but they will accept scores and they may or may not use it for admissions and/or scholarship qualifications. Test Blind schools assess students holistically and don't require and/or accept test scores because they are not factored into the decision-making process.

When should we have our ACT/SAT tests finished?

We recommend the completion of tests by the completion of first semester Junior Year, at the latest.

How often should I take the ACT/SAT?

Looking at the laws of probability, you want to take the test at least 3 times. The goal is to take the tests early and often

When should we start planning for college?

At the latest, you want to start planning around 7th or 8th grade to ensure you start HS on the best foot.

FAQs

What are standardized application systems?

Standardized application portals allow students to apply to multiple schools with a single application. Instead of filling out eight different applications, you can simply fill out one and submit it to each college.

The Coalition Application is accepted by more than 90 institutions. The platform includes "The Locker," a private space for you to collect and organize materials throughout high school that you might want to share with colleges and universities.

The Common Application is a standardized application used by nearly 700 colleges. Each year, nearly a million students use the Common Application to submit over 4 million applications.

The Universal College Application is accepted by more than 30 colleges and universities. You can register as an applicant in order to start applying.

The Common Black Application is accepted by 57 historically black colleges and universities for a nominal flat fee of $20.

Be aware that you may need to submit additional or separate documents to some colleges. You also still need to pay individual application fees for each college.

Do I need to be admitted to a college before I can apply for financial aid?

No. You can submit the Free Application for Federal Student Aid (FAFSA) and the College Service Scholarship PROFILE (CSS PROFILE) any time after October 1. But Note, you do need to be admitted to receive financial aid.

We make too much money to qualify for Financial Aid, why should we fill out the FAFSA?

There are various institutional, and government funded scholarships and loans that have nothing to do with income. If you don't complete the FAFSA, you won't be considered for those funding opportunities. The FAFSA is also required for many state-based college financial aid programs.

Is there a limit to the number of years I can get financial aid?

There are specific limits for federal financial aid programs. First time borrowers of subsidized loans are limited to a maximum time of 150% of the length of the student's program. This means that those in a four-year program are limited to six years of loans while those in two-year programs are limited to three years of loans. Pell Grants are limited to the equivalent of six years of funding. Students who receive Pell Grants are allowed 600% of Lifetime Eligibility Use (LEU). See the Federal Student Aid website for updates and more details

Congratulations
Hi Five College Bound Scholar!

You finished the guide, Congratulations! Putting in the work to outline your profile, goals, and future plans are necessary for activating your ability to go to college for free. Now, this doesn't mean you stop or slow down; you must keep moving forward.

To take your actions to the next level, here are your next steps.

Create a LinkedIn Profile using the information in this guide.

Identify people, schools, and organizations connected to your future goals, submit friend requests, and start engaging and following.

Identify at least three connections you can ask to write and publish recommendations on you within LinkedIn

Identify at least 3 to 5 people you can target to write letters of recommendations that provide specifics about how great you are. You will use these for scholarships and college applications

Apply for scholarships

Create a Targeted School List (10 to 15 schools) and start following them on LinkedIn, Twitter, IG, FB, etc.

If you are an HS Senior, apply for all targeted colleges between Aug and December 15th.

JOIN OUR FACEBOOK COMMUNITY

f www.facebook.com/college4free

Learn more about becoming a Money Magnet by connecting with us and joining the community

Create a Short Video or Fun Post Showing how you completed the planner or benefited from the use of the planner on any of our social media networks, tag us and use hashtag **#GettingAFullRide** for a chance to win a prize.

instagram.com/iamcoachtwill

Youtube.com/CoachTwill

crushcollegedebt.com

www.ingramcontent.com/pod-product-compliance
Lightning Source LLC
Chambersburg PA
CBHW040301100426
42811CB00011B/1329